MEDIA LITERACY™

ACCURACY IN MEDIA

MEGAN FROMM, Ph.D.

rosen publishing's
rosen
central®

NEW YORK

Published in 2015 by The Rosen Publishing Group, Inc.
29 East 21st Street, New York, NY 10010

First Edition

Library of Congress Cataloging-in-Publication Data

Fromm, Megan.
Accuracy in media/Megan Fromm.—First edition.
    pages cm.—(Media literacy)
Includes bibliographical references and index.
ISBN 978-1-4777-8070-1 (library bound)
1. Journalistic ethics—Juvenile literature. I. Title.
PN4797.F76 2015
174'.907–dc23

2014009986

Manufactured in Malaysia

CONTENTS

INTRODUCTION

Each year, the American Society of News Editors publishes a newsroom census—a detailed look at how many journalists make up America's media entourage and whether that number is growing or shrinking. Not surprisingly, the overall trend has been a downward spiral, from 52,600 full-time daily journalists in 2008 to only 38,000 in 2012.

At the same time, the number of web logs, or blogs, has risen drastically. Blogs are the most common tool for self-publishing in today's digital age. Blog search engine Technorati listed more than 1.3 million blogs in its directory and described the blogging medium as among the top five "most trustworthy" sources for consumers.

Another common blogging platform, WordPress, boasted almost seventy-five million blogs hosted through its site during the same time. That number has likely increased dramatically, even as you read this paragraph. Tumblr, a microblogging platform designed to allow users to publish in short, almost Twitter-like entries, has almost 170 million blogs registered.

Granted, some of these blogs may be defunct or rarely used, but the sheer amount of self-publishers in the world is staggering. Add in collaborative

Blogs are one of many new forms of media. Websites formatted for mobile devices, such as tablets and smartphones, are changing how journalists develop and publish stories.

media spaces, such as Wikipedia, and the amount of user-generated, self-published content on the Internet increases daily. In light of this reality, perhaps the recent decrease in the number of professional journalists is somewhat understandable.

Quite simply, every man, women, and child with Internet access can become a publisher or portray themselves as a journalist. This reality has made distinguishing credible online sources incredibly difficult, and at times, nearly impossible.

WHAT IS A PROFESSIONAL JOURNALIST?

What does it really take to consider oneself a journalist? How do we distinguish real reporters and editors from amateur journalists with a platform? And what truly makes someone "professional"? These are nuanced questions, but they strike at the heart of a consumer's quest to trust information and sources. Scholars, professors, lawyers, judges, and yes, journalists themselves have all tried to articulate exactly what qualities define a journalist.

CHANGING TECHNOLOGIES

The changing nature of publishing over the last century is partially to blame for the confusion over who is a journalist. Historically, journalists were often distinguished by the kind of information they provided—the facts they gathered about people, events, and policies generally held a unique public service value. That is, people used the information these journalists provided to help make better, more informed decisions about many facets of their lives.

Yemeni women use cameras and cell phones to document a protest against Ali Abdullah Saleh. The leader's thirty-three-year rule ended with immunity after an uprising in which hundreds were killed.

Because ink, paper, and the mechanical printing press were a pricey commodity once possessed only by the wealthy elite, printers were quite judicious about what made the cut in their newspapers, magazines, or newsletters. As technology developed and printing became more accessible to the layman, the type of information printed also expanded.

Ink, paper, and a warehouse of mechanical presses are now no longer barriers to entry for would-be publishers. And if everyone can publish, is anyone really a journalist? Thankfully, just as history complicates the matter, it can also provide some clarity for the future of the profession.

THE DEFINITION OF "JOURNALIST"

In 2013, media lawyer and professor Jonathon Peters and Fulbright Scholar Edson Tandoc attempted to extrapolate a legal definition of "journalist" based on contemporary media law[1] and scholarly research. They found that most conceptions of a journalist stress a few distinct characteristics:

1. **Output**—What, exactly, is the person creating? Journalists output mostly news, but opinion, when properly identified as such, also counts.
2. **Social role**—Is the person acting as a gatekeeper or advocate of information?
3. **Ethics**—Is the person exhibiting "benchmarks of a professional practice" that demonstrate his or her commitment to outcomes such as truth and accuracy?

Based on their research, they developed this definition of a professional journalist: "A journalist is someone employed to regularly engage in gathering, processing, and disseminating (activities) news and information (output) to serve the public interest (social role)."

Do you notice anything problematic about that definition? As the authors point out, this disqualifies bloggers, citizen journalists, and other self-publishers from being considered professional journalists. In fact, Peters and Tandoc go so far as to say this definition might be unwise because it fails to accurately account for the contributions of new media and new forms of journalism.

Thomas Jefferson was a proponent of a free press because he believed it helped citizens keep a watchful eye on the government and share responsibility for creating a democratic nation.

JOURNALISM AND THE FOUNDING FATHERS

Turning to America's founding fathers, such as Thomas Jefferson and James Madison, we can better understand their vision for "the press." In a letter he wrote in 1789 [2], Jefferson explained why an informed citizenry is so vital to a democracy: "Whenever the people are well informed, they can be trusted with their own government; that whenever things get so far wrong as to attract their notice, they may be relied on to set them to rights." Journalism, then, is a means to effective self-governance in an elected republic.

Similarly, Madison believed that the press would serve as a watchdog over the government, alerting citizens if their elected officials were exerting too much authoritarian control. He once wrote: "A popular government, without popular information, or the means of acquiring it, is but a prologue to a farce or a tragedy; or perhaps both. Knowledge will forever govern ignorance; and a people who mean to be their own governors must arm

In the early 1970s, *Washington Post* reporters Carl Bernstein (left) and Bob Woodward broke one of the most important stories in modern journalism: Watergate.

themselves with the power which knowledge gives."[3] Journalists, then, are the middlemen who arm the people with the power of knowledge.

Undoubtedly, there is value in a vast spectrum of content—political, cultural, religious, social, literary, and scientific. In the age of digital mass media, we cannot underestimate the power of these types of content. However, in honoring the best intentions of the founding fathers of our country and upholding the needs of our citizens, we can see that true journalism—and the journalists who practice the profession—still hold an important place in our democracy.

CHAPTER TWO

BALANCING DIGITAL IDENTITIES

The ability to easily create a digital identity is one reason why it is more difficult today than fifty years ago to decipher who is a journalist. With just a few clicks and strategic thinking, we can compose entire online personalities, personas, and professional reputations that are entirely fabricated.

On the flip side, those who truly are professional journalists are being subject to scrutiny in ways never experienced before. A journalist's entire digital identity—social media posts, photos, etc.—is now easily linked to his or her professional work, blurring the line between personal and private. In some ways, this means today's journalists have to work even harder to demonstrate their professionalism.

More than a handful of reporters and editors have fallen from grace when their digital persona was unfavorably tied to their professional identity. In 2013, an Alabama television reporter was fired for comments she posted on her personal blog that related to her work on-air. Similarly, in 2012, the

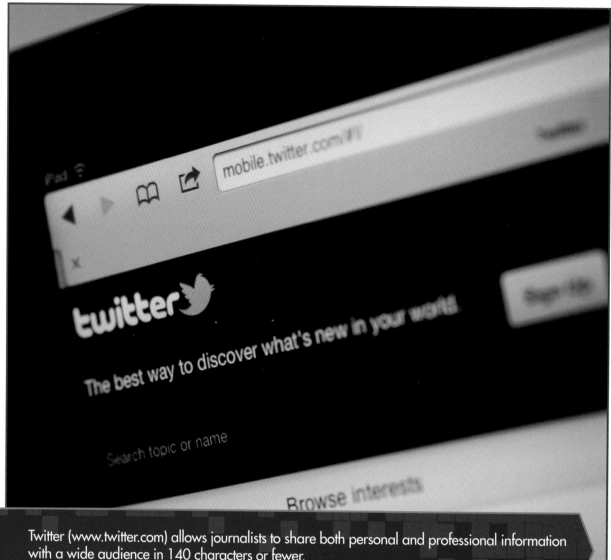

Twitter (www.twitter.com) allows journalists to share both personal and professional information with a wide audience in 140 characters or fewer.

website Politico suspended a reporter for publishing a vulgar tweet, or Twitter message, about politician Mitt Romney. An *Arizona Daily Star* reporter was fired in 2010 for posting potentially offensive comments to his personal Twitter page that joked about Tucson, Arizona's, crime rate.

In each case, the publishers defended their decisions to terminate the journalists' employment, citing concern over public trust and damaged

likely to see an advertisement for a similar product on your social media website tomorrow.

Search engines work exactly the same way. So search engines such as Google, Bing, and Yahoo! are using information stored in your web browser to customize the kind of information you see in each search based off all your previous search activity. Unconvinced? Try sitting with a friend and searching for the same phrase on two different computers. Chances are, your results will be only somewhat similar.

Additionally, search engines use algorithms to generate responses for each individual user based on the IP address and recent web activity. This algorithm means that you might not actually see the most accurate, truthful, or thorough results when you search for information. Instead, you're likely to see a list of results for websites that the search engine's algorithm has deemed most tailored to your past searches and recent online activity. This somewhat circular process can mean that your own political, cultural, social, religious, and economic perspectives are only being reinforced by search engine results. In short, these search engines display what they think you want to see.

Similarly, search engines use algorithms to rank the websites on each search return. In other words, the order in which you see websites on a search results page is based largely on how popular that search engine determines each site to be. Popularity, or page rank, is based on a number of factors, but one of the most common considerations is how many times other sites or pages link to the site in question. This can often mean that the most popular sites only continue to become more popular because they are constantly returned as results in search engine queries. Less popular websites, according to this kind of algorithm, are unlikely to rise higher in page rank.

You might wonder what, if anything, is the big deal about a search engine customizing results or returning only those results that tend to be most popular. In a world where information is also a commercial product, it matters a great deal whether consumers are exposed to a variety of sources and perspectives in their online search process.

Considering all these factors, you can see why a consumer might need help in the information verification process. Just because a search engine returns a relevant result does not necessarily mean it offers the best or most accurate information. So, how should consumers proceed to better evaluate the accuracy of their sources? Like any good reporter, the simplest answer is to dig, dig, dig until you have solid evidence that information and sources are credible. Often, that means turning to the experts.

EXPERT SOURCES

Expert sources are among the most common sources of information in news reports and on the Internet. Generally, we think of doctors, lawyers, politicians, researchers, and experienced practitioners in general to be expert sources. However, just because a person has a degree or perceived access to information does not mean he or she is necessarily credible or in a position to know certain facts. Expert sources should be evaluated as judiciously as any other source to ensure that he or she is reliable and truthful.

When considering whether a person is truly an expert source and if this source's information can be trusted, start with these questions:

1. Does he/she provide evidence of experience and expertise in this area?
2. Do others in the field validate his/her approach or perspective?
3. Have experts, groups, or institutions in the field ever censured or reprimanded him/her?
4. Does this person's livelihood depend on the information or perspective being provided?
5. What personal or professional stake does this person have in making sure you see his/her point of view?

Sometimes, deciphering whether an expert source has financial ties to the information he or she provides is key to evaluating credibility. Many expert sources hail from research universities. And while many research universities

Scientist and researcher Andrew Wakefield has been accused of manipulating the results of a study that claimed a link between childhood vaccines and autism. In 2010, his findings were retracted and deemed fabricated.

conduct and publish top-notch, groundbreaking research, some unfortunately rely on the funding and research agendas of financial partners to guide their work. This begs the addition of a final expert source question: Who is funding this person's work, and could this undermine his or her findings?

Dr. Andrew Wakefield, the infamous doctor who claimed to have linked autism with various childhood vaccines, is a relevant example of a non-credible expert source. Despite numerous other researchers' inability to ever duplicate Wakefield's findings that vaccinations led to autism, his work was cited repeatedly for decades as an argument against vaccinating children. Mainstream and celebrity media often reported on his work, but other scientists found major flaws in his methodology and conclusions.[4]

Finally, in 2010, the U.K. journal that originally published Wakefield's research filed a retraction, saying the findings were fraudulent. However, popular sentiment abroad and in the United States has yet to catch up; a 2011 NPR poll found that 21 percent of respondents still believe there is a link between autism and childhood vaccinations.[5] This is just one example of how vital it is for consumers and journalists to carefully evaluate the claims of even the most expert sources.

Even without direct access to a source, consumers can take steps to analyze a website's credibility. Keeping in mind the potential for an Internet search to return biased or incomplete information, consumers can use the online evaluation tips in the next chapter to start analyzing websites. When the source is unclear—that is, when the originator of information is a website or webpage with no obvious author—evaluating the website as a whole might be the only option.

CHAPTER THREE

EVALUATING WEBSITES FOR CREDIBILITY

Not long ago, only the technologically elite understood how websites worked; only coders or engineers could create websites that looked remotely legitimate and functioned as they should. Today, however, creating a professional-looking website is as easy as selecting a template from an online platform and filling in the information. This can make it even more difficult to decipher professional, credible websites from those that aim to misinform.

One of the benefits of publishing online is the ability to tell a story from multiple perspectives. With no space constraints, websites can devote nuanced coverage to complex stories.

Of course, just because a website *looks* credible doesn't make it so. According to Jonathan Stray on www.niemanlab.org, some recent recent studies have shown that websites that are visually pleasing are assumed to be more credible even when the content might suggest otherwise. When it comes to web design and information credibility, it is really easy to judge a book by its cover, so consumers should take care to evaluate websites from a holistic perspective.

JUDGING WEBSITES

There are certain professional standards for design, usability, content, and function that, when misapplied or overlooked entirely, can give consumers reason to be wary. Using these four areas and a list of related questions, consumers can easily evaluate how credible a website might be. We'll explore each of these four areas in more detail.

DESIGN
- Does the site use professional-looking colors and fonts?
- Is the design simple and purposeful, or chaotic and overwhelming?
- Is there a clear and/or prominent logo that easily identifies the site's affiliation?

USABILITY
- Does the site have tabs that are easy to navigate, including a home page and contact section?
- Is the format of the page easy to navigate, including the length of the scroll?
- Are all the links active?
- Is there a "home" button or other menu option to easily navigate to the main page?

- Do the pages provide manageable amounts of information, or must the user scroll many times to access everything on one page?
- Are there pop-up ads or other intrusive elements that disrupt use?

CONTENT

- Is there an "About Us" section or a "Contact Us" section with addresses, phone numbers, and e-mail addresses?
- Is there a wide range of content that explores information from a variety of angles?
- Are sentences grammatically correct, and is everything spelled correctly?
- Is the tone appropriate for the content? Is it clear whether the information is meant to be neutral or biased toward a specific perspective?
- Is the information provided supported by multiple sources, both primary and secondary?

FUNCTION

- Can you find author information for each piece of content? Is contact information included?
- Does the site link out to other sources and websites that are related or that can supplement the information provided?
- Does the site provide information about when it was most recently updated?
- Would a novice user, or someone without much topic knowledge, be able to navigate the site to find specific information?
- Can you tell what the overall function of the website is? Is it to inform, persuade, sell and market a product, discuss, or promote?

(continued on the next page)

(continued from the previous page)

Many different organizations even offer website credibility checklists—a list of points you can evaluate to determine an overall ranking of a website's credibility. Used with the questions above, these lists can help consumers more easily sift through online fact and fiction. However, these questions might not be as helpful if the website in question is a user-generated website, or wiki. Often, these kinds of websites require a different consumer approach to determine what information is most credible.

Many major news websites, like the *New York Times*, *Washington Post*, and CNN, demonstrate a clear function to provide news even if they also provide other content.

USER-GENERATED RESOURCES

Websites such as Wikipedia that rely entirely on contributions from users present a unique set of problems for determining the credibility of the information. First, there is no longer a singular source to evaluate because information is coming from many contributors. Second, most contributors to these kinds of community-edited websites are anonymous or profile-based, meaning consumers may not have access to any real identifying information. And finally, because these sites are often large and unwieldy (Wikipedia currently boasts more than four million pages), isolating errors in fact or context can prove almost impossible.

One of the best ways to assess credibility for user-generated sites is to consider the contribution and posting policies of these platforms. Sites with moderators who evaluate submissions before they are posted could be more reliable because of the extra filter. Websites with active take-down policies, like Wikipedia, might also have higher levels of accuracy than static websites that are updated infrequently.

Because user-generated resources are more difficult to analyze for credibility and bias, consumers should consider how transparent these websites are in their policies and practices. To use Wikipedia again as an example, the website advocates a strict conflict-of-interest policy that directs contributors not to edit or contribute simply based on their own interests or benefit. In fact, the Wikipedia policies page lists many policies for its content standards, including the desire for neutral points of view, verifiability, and what actions to take when disputing content. These kinds of guidelines, while not a guarantee of accurate information, indicate a desire to maintain high levels of credibility and reliability.

At times, user-generated sites can actually function like professional news media, providing real-time facts as they unfold. For instance, the community-generated site Reddit provided some of the most accurate and comprehensive play-by-play accounts during the Aurora, Colorado, movie theater shooting in 2012.

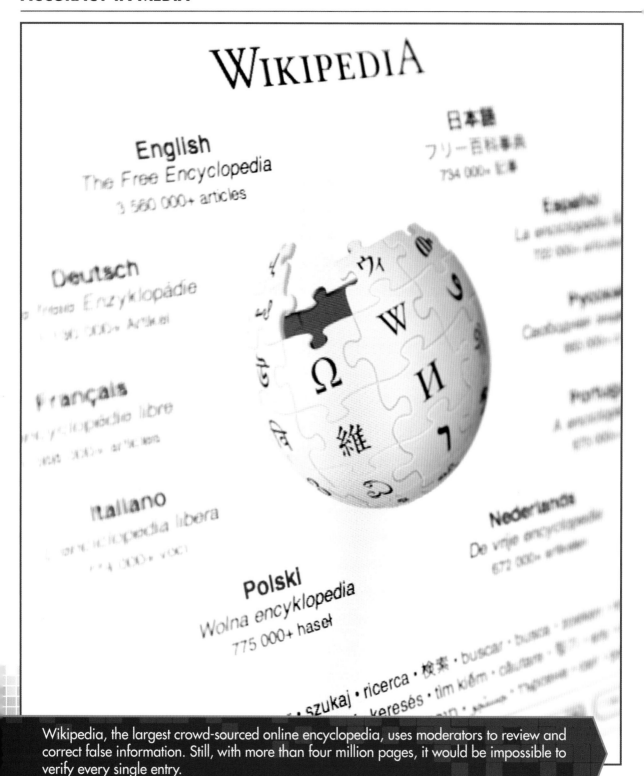

Wikipedia, the largest crowd-sourced online encyclopedia, uses moderators to review and correct false information. Still, with more than four million pages, it would be impossible to verify every single entry.

Not only did the Reddit website provide a list of police activity, traffic, and safety information, but the community of users were even self-moderating. For example, one entry on the shooting page gave the make, model, and license plate of a car outside the movie theater during the immediate aftermath of the shooting. When other users remarked that identifying the car could put the safety of the owner at risk, the information was removed from the site.

Not all Reddit pages and users demonstrate this level of care and consideration for facts, however. During the Boston marathon bombing in 2013, users posted cell phone images from the scene to facilitate a crowdsourced investigation of sorts. Ultimately, two teenagers who were not involved with the bombing were mistakenly identified as potential bombers. Their lives were threatened, their reputations were harmed, and much-needed energy and attention were diverted from other leads. The damage to these individuals' name and character is not easily undone, since their digital identity is now forever tied to the Boston marathon bombing.

What happened as a result of the "citizen investigation" during the Boston marathon bombing prompted Reddit staffers to issue an apology for the witch hunt it created, stating that it hopes the organization will be more sensitive about its own power.

For these reasons and more, consumer participation in news gathering can be both harmful and helpful. If citizens employ their own code of ethics when contributing to user-generated websites, the quality of information provided could become more reliable. But when the need to publish first outweighs concern for the truth, communities and people are hurt in the process. In these cases, consumers must be proactive and cautious about what information they choose to trust from crowdsourced websites.

CHAPTER FOUR

ATTRIBUTION AND ANONYMOUS SOURCES

By now, you've likely noticed that a large part of determining what information is credible relates directly to the source of that information. Correct and dependable attribution, or assigning information to a specific source, is one of the most important tasks of a journalist. Occasionally, journalists use anonymous sources to access information to which they otherwise would not be privy. While at times necessary, the use of anonymous sources makes it especially burdensome to determine credibility.

When a journalist uses an anonymous source, he or she takes on the responsibility of vetting that information. To publish from an anonymous source essentially means the journalist takes credit for that information being right or wrong. This is a heavy burden to bear, and relying on anonymous sources too often can lead to the loss of consumer trust and can even damage the reputation of the journalist.

The best approach a media consumer can take when reading information that comes from an anonymous source is to be skeptical and do his or her own homework about the topic. Here are some key questions to ask if a story you are reading contains an anonymous source:

1. Why would the reporter have needed to use an anonymous source? Is there a justifiable or acceptable rationale?

2. Who else could have provided this information on the record?

3. Are any other publications or news media relying on anonymous sources?

4. What risk to the source is there in divulging this information? Is the information important enough to warrant using an anonymous source?

Often, the answers to these questions can give consumers a much clearer perspective on how credible an anonymous source might be. Given recent instances in which reporters have come under fire for anonymous sources, the average consumer should recognize that most professional journalists do not take lightly the use of anonymous sources in their reporting.

Organizations such as the Society of Professional Journalists have specific guidelines for when using anonymous sources is appropriate. These guidelines require a high burden of proof from anonymous sources. In other words, when a journalist uses an unnamed source, he or she still has to verify that information with another source. In general, these kinds of sources are used only when there is concern about the physical or emotional well-being of the source, that he or she may be harmed in some way if identified for the information provided. Knowing this, news consumers should assume that if an anonymous source is being used for basic or non-vital information, there is reason to be skeptical.

FRIENDLY INFORMATION AND FALSE SECURITY

Today, many online consumers receive news and information from a combination of sources, including professional media, social media, and friends via e-mail or other networks. As humans, we tend to assume that our digital network of friends would do us no harm—that is, they wouldn't provide us with information that is false or misleading. Unfortunately, because passing along articles, videos, and images is so easy, many media consumers unknowingly forward misinformation.

When Hurricane Sandy hit in October, 2012, Twitter was inundated with supposed images from the storm. Those images were tweeted and re-tweeted by citizen users and even professional media. Given the chaotic nature of the event, many of the photos weren't vetted for accuracy before they were republished.

In the end, many Twitter users did not know that they were seeing, responding to, and passing along fake photos. One of the most infamous fake photos was actually a composite image from a Hollywood movie about a disastrous storm.

WHEN CONTEXT COMPROMISES CREDIBILITY

As this section indicates, quality journalism is based largely on the quality of sources used. However, it's important for consumers to know that sometimes, in the quest for credibility, the very process that helps journalists be most accurate might also compromise the context and truth value of the information consumers ultimately receive. How? By lending too much

When Hurricane Sandy hit the East Coast, thousands of images circulated on social media. Unfortunately, some of the photos that received the most attention were fake, manipulated with computer software.

credit to "expert" sources. To explain, let's examine one of the most interesting examples of compromised credibility and balance in recent media history: climate change.

A controversial topic, climate change is hotly debated in scientific communities around the world. Much of the mass media coverage of climate change has followed suit, aiming to present multiple opinions from myriad expert sources. However, in doing so, the media have actually amplified less credible voices while muffling those experts with significant authority on the topic.[6] This practice is known as false balance, or when two contradictory opinions are presented to appear equal in a he-said-she-said approach.

In reality, most scientists agree that a fundamental shift in the overall climate of Earth is presently occurring. In fact, among climate change experts, a 2013 study in the *Environmental Research Letters* journal suggests there is as much as a 97 percent agreement that humans are contributing to global warming in some way.[7] Exactly how much is man-made, and how much is a result of natural atmospheric and geologic fluctuations is up for debate, but media coverage has largely shifted this reality to portray a level of discord or skepticism that many scientists say just does not exist.

Fairness and Accuracy in Reporting, a progressive media watchdog and think tank, conducted its own analysis of media coverage of climate change and found similar results: The media were creating a false balance of ideas

Some breaking news, like the story of the killing of Osama bin Laden on the *Los Angeles Times* website, needs relatively little context to explain what happened. Other topics, like climate change, require more information to capture the true scope.

by posing "dueling scientists" that disagreed on what exactly was happening to Earth's temperature and natural weather cycles.[8]

Now, in an effort to rectify this false balance, some media outlets are banning letters to the editor that disagree with scientific claims of climate change. In October 2013, the *Los Angeles Times* announced it would no longer publish letters to the editor in its print edition from "climate change deniers" in an effort to keep errors in fact from appearing on the opinion pages.[9] Letters Editor Paul Thornton explained the decision on the *Times'* website: "Saying 'there's no sign humans have caused climate change' is not stating an opinion, it's asserting a factual inaccuracy."

While Thornton's move may prove to be a bold step toward the ideal journalism of verification discussed earlier, it does shut the door for public debate—a much-praised function of traditional media.

In response to the *Times'* policy change, other major newspapers weighed in regarding their own letters to the editor standards. Vincent Carroll, editorial page editor at the *Denver Post*, wrote in an editorial response that he is "reluctant to shut down reader discussion on issues in which most scientists may share similar views. Where would it end? What other debates raging among our readers do the arbiters of truth believe we should silence?"

CHAPTER FIVE

CREDIBILITY AND PERSONAL BIAS

While credibility often appears to many media consumers as an outside force or something beyond their control, the element of personal bias can play a significant role in identifying and appreciating a source's credibility. In fact, our own deeply rooted perspectives on high-profile topics such as politics or religion can even keep us from recognizing credible, balanced information.

In the world of mass-media research, some scholars focus exclusively on these so-called theories of media effects. Often using a series of controlled experiments, media effects researchers can determine consumers' own preconceived attitudes toward the media they consume. Then they can isolate and discuss how this could affect consumers' beliefs about concepts such as media credibility and fairness.

THE BRIDGE TRAGEDY · MURDOCH'S WAR PLAN

Newsweek

August 13, 2007 : $4.95

newsweek.com

Global Warming Is A Hoax.*

PHOTOGRAPH BY SOHO—ESA-NASA

* Or so claim well-funded naysayers who still reject the overwhelming evidence of climate change. Inside the denial machine. By Sharon Begley

NASA image of the Sun

Debate about the cause and effect of climate change is one area in which media coverage, in an attempt to remain neutral, might actually distort scientific consensus.

35

Dubbed the "hostile media effect," this theory suggests that a person with strong feelings on an issue will automatically perceive media to be biased against his or her cause, even if the media coverage has been neutral. This theory has significant consequences for understanding credibility. If we are preconditioned to think the media are always biased against the issues most important to us, we are unlikely to recognize credible, contextual information even if it were right in front of us.

The most helpful takeaway from the dozens of research studies about this theory is that it teaches us that, as consumers, we are not as smart or discerning as we hope we are when it comes to the quality of the media we seek and believe. The Nieman Journalism Lab at Harvard University more succinctly describes why understanding and recognizing this phenomenon matters: "We might like to think of ourselves as impartial judges of credibility and fairness, but the evidence says otherwise."[10]

EXPLORING CREDIBILITY

Together with your classmates or on your own complete the following exercises to explore credibility and the personal biases you might bring to the table when consuming media.

1. Find a website credibility checklist online or use the questions in this chapter to evaluate your favorite news and entertainment sites. Explain and discuss your findings.
2. Using your local or regional newspaper, look for uses of anonymous sources, and then evaluate whether you think the use was justified based on the facts outlined in the previous chapter.
3. Take a few minutes to consider your own biases about certain topics. Would you be able to identify a credible source and believe him or her even if the view contradicted your own?

OWNING OUR VIEWS, OPENING OUR MINDS

With all the forces that seem to work against establishing and maintaining journalistic integrity, it is easy for media consumers to feel as if no one, or no media, is trustworthy. This is a cynical and destructive

With ever-increasing options for news and information, it's easy for consumers to feel overwhelmed and potentially helpless in discerning what is truthful. Media literacy is an ongoing process to help empower consumers.

approach, and one that is likely to only perpetuate a feeling of power-lessness against the media that constantly surround us.

Instead of seeing obstacles to credibility as impenetrable roadblocks, media-literate citizens view them as opportunities to learn, grow, and expand their beliefs. Think of it as resistance training for your mind—the more you challenge your own thoughts and perceptions by critically consuming and evaluating a wide variety of media, the stronger your mind grows and the more supported your positions will be. Most impor-tant, adopting even the most basic media literacy practices helps consumers become more savvy news readers, viewers, and listeners. In turn, this could challenge news producers and journalists to maintain only the highest standards of truth and accuracy.

ALGORITHM A mathematical process often used in computer programming to help define and guide specific operations.

ANONYMOUS SOURCE A person who remains unidentified in the news media.

ATTRIBUTION The method by which a source is identified or by which facts and information are assigned to the person who provided them.

BIAS A disposition or prejudice in favor of a certain idea, person, or perspective. Many media outlets are believed to have bias toward a specific political party.

COOKIE A small piece of data sent from a website to a user's browser, where it is stored and provides personalized data to the website during each subsequent visit.

CREDIBILITY The quality of being believed or trusted. In regard to news media, this especially relates to how reliable users perceive a given publication to be.

CROWDSOURCE In reference to news media, this typically means to gather information from many people, generally unpaid, who participate by offering information or personal opinion.

EXPERT SOURCE A person who, by education, experience, or practice, has intricate and detailed knowledge of a certain subject matter.

FALSE BALANCE Sometimes called structural bias or informational bias, this occurs when opposing viewpoints are presented as being equally valid or truthful.

HOSTILE MEDIA EFFECT The media theory that, regardless of whether a story or publication is neutral, readers will still believe it to be against their personal cause or perceptions.

IP ADDRESS A unique string of numbers assigned to each device connected over a network.

JOURNALISM OF VERIFICATION A systematic approach to fact-finding detailed in *The Elements of Journalism*, by Bill Kovach and Tom Rosenstiel.

MICROBLOGGING An approach to blogging or self-publishing in which the word count of entries or posts is drastically limited.

TAKE-DOWN POLICY A website's written standard for removing inaccurate information.

TUMBLR A microblogging platform that allows users to post entries in short, character-limited forms.

USABILITY The ease of use of a website. Usability can affect perceptions of credibility.

WORDPRESS A popular blogging platform that allows users to create their own websites.

FOR MORE INFORMATION

American Society of News Editors (ASNE)
209 Reynolds Journalism Institute
Missouri School of Journalism
Columbia, MO 65211
(573) 884-2405
Website: http://www.asne.org
ASNE is tasked with helping journalists refine their craft and protect the free
    flow of information.

Fairness & Accuracy In Reporting (FAIR)
104 West 27th Street, Suite 10B
New York, NY 10001
(212) 633-6700
Website: http://www.fair.org
FAIR is a national media watchdog group that publishes criticism of media
    bias and censorship.

Journalism Education Association (JEA)
Kansas State University
103 Kedzie Hall
Manhattan, KS 66506-1505
(866) 532-5532
Website: http://www.jea.org
JEA is the largest professional association for secondary journalism teachers
    and scholastic media advisers.

Media Matters
P.O. Box 52155
Washington, DC 20091
(202) 756-4100
Website: http://www.mediamatters.org

Media Matters describes itself as a progressive center dedicated to monitoring and correcting conservative misinformation in the U.S. media.

National Association for Media Literacy Education (NAMLE)
10 Laurel Hill Drive
Cherry Hill, NJ 08003
(888) 775-2652
Website: http://www.namle.net
NAMLE is a national membership organization dedicated to helping citizens of all ages learn media literacy skills.

Nieman Journalism Lab
Nieman Foundation at Harvard University
1 Francis Avenue
Cambridge, MA 02138
(617) 496-0168
Website: http://www.niemanlab.org
Nieman Lab aims to help journalists navigate online reporting by providing research and insight regarding journalism innovation in a digital age.

Pew Research Center State of the News Media Survey
1615 L Street NW, Suite 700
Washington, DC 20036
(202) 419-4300
Website: http://www.stateofthemedia.org
The State of the News Media Survey is conducted yearly by the Pew Research Center. The survey tracks trends in technology, readership, newsroom size, and other aspects of the journalism industry.

ProPublica
One Exchange Plaza
55 Broadway, 23rd Floor

New York, NY 10006
(212) 514-5250
Website: http://www.propublica.org
A nonprofit, independent news organization that focuses on investigative
journalism, ProPublica is funded through grants and philanthropic
donations.

Society for Professional Journalists (SJP)
Eugene S. Pulliam National Journalism Center
3909 N. Meridian Street
Indianapolis, IN 46208
Website: http://www.spj.org
The largest membership organization for professional journalists, SPJ helps
support journalists' quest for freedom of information and the First
Amendment.

WEBSITES

Because of the changing nature of Internet links, Rosen Publishing has developed an online list of websites related to the subject of this book. This site is updated regularly. Please use this link to access the list:

http://www.rosenlinks.com/MEDL/Accur

FOR FURTHER READING

Alterman, Eric. *What Liberal Media? The Truth About Bias and the News.* New York, NY: Basic Books, 2008.

Biagi, Shirley. *Media/Impact: An Introduction to Mass Media.* Stamford, CT: Cengage Learning, 2012.

Boczkowski, Pablo J., and Eugenia Mitchelstein. *The News Gap: When the Information Preferences of the Media and the Public Diverge.* Cambridge, MA: MIT Press, 2013.

Briggs, Mark. *Journalism Next: A Practical Guide to Digital Reporting and Publishing.* Washington, DC: CQ Press, 2010.

Folkenflik, David. *Page One: Inside the New York Times and the Future of Journalism.* New York, NY: PublicAffairs, 2011.

Groseclose, Tim. *Left Turn: How Liberal Media Bias Distorts the American Mind.* New York, NY: St. Martin's Press, 2011.

Harrower, Tim. *Inside Reporting.* 3rd ed. New York, NY: McGraw-Hill, 2012.

Jenkins, Henry. *Convergence Culture: Where Old & New Media Collide.* New York, NY: New York University, 2006.

Kovach, Bill, and Tom Rosenstiel. *Blur: How to Know What's True in the Age of Information Overload.* New York, NY: Bloomsbury, 2010.

Kovach, Bill, and Tom Rosenstiel. *The Elements of Journalism.* New York, NY: Three Rivers, 2007.

Rosenberg, Scott. *Say Everything: How Blogging Began, What It's Becoming, and Why It Matters.* New York, NY: Crown Publishers, 2009.

1 Peters, Jonathan, and Edson C. Tandoc Jr. "People Who Aren't Really Reporters at All, Who Have No Professional Qualifications: Defining a Journalist and Deciding Who May Claim the Privileges." *NYU Journal of Legislation and Public Policy,* March 2013. Retrieved July 14, 2014 (http://www.nyujlpp.org/wp-content/uploads/2013/03/Peters-Tandoc-Quorum-2013.pdf).

2 Jefferson, Thomas. "Selected Quotations from the Thomas Jefferson Papers." Library of Congress. Retrieved July 14, 2014 (http://memory.loc.gov/ammem/collections/jefferson_papers/mtjquote.html).

3 The Founders' Constitution. "Epilogue: Securing the Republic." Retrieved July 14, 2014 (http://press-pubs.uchicago.edu/founders/documents/v1ch18s35.html).

4 American Academy of Pediatrics. "Autism and Andrew Wakefield." Retrieved July 14, 2014 (http://www2.aap.org/immunization/families/autismwakefield.html).

5 Hensley, Scott. "Worries About Autism Link Still Hang Over Vaccines." NPR, September 29, 2011. Retrieved July 14, 2014 (http://www.npr.org/blogs/health/2011/09/29/140928470/worries-about-autism-link-still-hang-over-vaccines).

6 Greenberg, Max, Denise Robbins, and Shauna Theel. "Study: Media Sowed Doubt in Coverage of UN Climate Report." Media Matters, October 10, 2013. Retrieved July 14, 2014 (http://mediamatters.org/research/2013/10/10/study-media-sowed-doubt-in-coverage-of-un-clima/196387).

7 Cook, John. "Quantifying the Consensus on Anthropogenic Global Warming in the Scientific Literature." IOP Science. Retrieved July 14, 2014 (http://iopscience.iop.org/1748-9326/8/2/024024).

8 Boykoff, Jules, and Maxwell Boykoff. "Journalistic Balance as Global Warming Bias." FAIR. Retrieved July 14, 2014 (http://fair.org/extra-online-articles/journalistic-balance-as-global-warming-bias).

9 Thornton, Paul. "On Letters from Climate-Change Deniers." LATimes.com. Retrieved July 14, 2014 (http://www.latimes.com/opinion/opinion-la/la-ol-climate-change-letters-20131008,0,871615.story#axzz2sGzePl78).

10 Stray, John. "How Do You Tell When the News Is Biased? It Depends on How You See Yourself." Nieman Journalism Lab. Retrieved July 14, 2014 (http://www.niemanlab.org/2012/06/how-do-you-tell-when-the-news-is-biased).

INDEX

A
advertisements, personalized, 15–17
algorithms, and search engines, 17
American Society of News Editors, 4
attribution, 28–29
autism and vaccines, controversy
surrounding, 20

B
Bing, 17
blogs/bloggers, 4, 8

C
Carroll, Vincent, 33
citizen journalists, 8
climate change, as example of compromised
credibility and balance, 31–33
collaborative media spaces, 4–5
context, when it compromises credibility,
30–33
cookies, 15–16

D
digital identities, balancing personal and
professional, 11–13

E
Elements of Journalism, The, 13

F
Facebook, 16
Fairness and Accuracy in Reporting, 32–33
false balance, 31–33
founding fathers, and journalism, 9–10

G
Google, 17
government, the press as watchdog of, 9–10

H
hostile media effect theory, 34–36

I
IP addresses, 14–15, 17

J
Jefferson, Thomas, 9
journalist, professional
deciphering who is, 11, 13
decrease in number of, 4, 5
definition of, 8
what it means to be a, 6–10, 11

K
Kovach, Bill, 13

M
Madison, James, 9–10
media effects, 34–36
misinformation, passing on, 30

N
Nieman Journalism Lab at Harvard
University, 36

P
personal bias, and credibility, 34–36
exercise for, 36

ABOUT THE AUTHOR

Megan Fromm is an assistant professor at Boise State University and faculty for the Salzburg Academy on Media & Global Change, a summer media literacy study-abroad program. She is also the professional support director for the Journalism Education Association.

Fromm received her Ph.D. in 2010 from the Philip Merrill College of Journalism at the University of Maryland. Her dissertation analyzed how news media frame student First Amendment court cases, particularly those involving freedom of speech and press. Her work and teaching centers on media law, scholastic journalism, media literacy, and media and democracy. She has also worked as a journalist and high school journalism teacher. Fromm has taught at Johns Hopkins University, Towson University, the University of Maryland, and the Newseum.

As a working journalist, Fromm won numerous awards, including the Society of Professional Journalists Sunshine Award and the Colorado Friend of the First Amendment Award. Fromm worked in student media through high school and college and interned at the Student Press Law Center in 2004. Her career in journalism began at Grand Junction High School (Grand Junction, Colorado), where she was a reporter and news editor for the award-winning student newspaper, the *Orange & Black*.

PHOTO CREDITS